SPOT 50
Rocks & Minerals

Steve Parker

Miles Kelly

First published in 2015 by Miles Kelly Publishing Ltd
Harding's Barn, Bardfield End Green, Thaxted, Essex, CM6 3PX, UK

2 4 6 8 10 9 7 5 3 1

Publishing Director Belinda Gallagher

Creative Director Jo Cowan

Editorial Director Rosie Neave

Senior Editor Sarah Parkin

Designer Rob Hale

Image Manager Liberty Newton

Production Manager Elizabeth Collins

Reprographics Stephan Davis, Jennifer Cozens, Thom Allaway

ISBN 978-1-78209-855-3

Printed in China

British Library Cataloguing-in-Publication Data
A catalogue record for this book is available from the British Library

ACKNOWLEDGEMENTS
The publishers would like to thank the following sources for the use of their photographs:
t = top, b = bottom, l = left, r = right, c = centre
Cover (front) Boris Sosnovyy/Shutterstock.com, (back) see below
Corbis 5(c) Floresco Productions/cultura; 8 Visuals Unlimited; 20 Gary Cook, Inc/Visuals Unlimited
Dreamstime.com 50(& cover) Miroslava Holasová iStockphoto.com 1 & 36 lissart
Science Photo Library 5(tl) Matteis/Look at sciences; 7 Photostock-Israel; 14 Mark A. Schneider; 31 Natural History Museum,
London; 43 Scientifica, Visuals Unlimited Shutterstock.com 4(top to bottom) dmitriyd, Vladimir Dokovski, carlosvelayos,
Vitaly Raduntsev, Tyler Boyes, paulrommer; 5(bl) Dawn Hudson; 6 Richard Peterson; 9 Ratchanat Bua-ngern;
10 Christopher Kolaczan; 11 Anneka; 12 farbled; 13 MarcelClemens; 15 Asya Babushkina; 16 Siim Sepp; 17 Vitaly Raduntsev;
18 Tyler Boyes; 19 Tyler Boyes; 21 Denis Radovanovic; 22 Stefano Cavoretto; 23 Siim Sepp; 24 Tyler Boyes;
25(& cover) Tyler Boyes; 26 Siim Sepp; 27 Tyler Boyes; 28 Bragin Alexey; 29 Siim Sepp; 30 Siim Sepp; 32 Massimiliano Gallo;
33 Tyler Boyes; 34 sokolenok; 35 Siim Sepp; 37(& cover) Tyler Boyes; 38 Tyler Boyes; 39 Siim Sepp; 40 kavring; 41 Siim Sepp;
42 Tyler Boyes; 44 Tyler Boyes; 45 Tyler Boyes; 46 antoni halim; 47 Siim Sepp; 48 Siim Sepp; 49 humbak; 51 Tyler Boyes;
52 michal812; 53 Tyler Boyes; 54 Tom Grundy; 55 Muellek Josef

Every effort has been made to acknowledge the source and copyright holder of each picture.
Miles Kelly Publishing apologizes for any unintentional errors or omissions.

Made with paper from a sustainable forest

www.mileskelly.net
info@mileskelly.net

CONTENTS

Tick the circles when you have spotted the specimens.

WHAT TO LOOK FOR

To identify rocks and minerals, you need to know how they look and feel. Here are some important features and how to describe them.

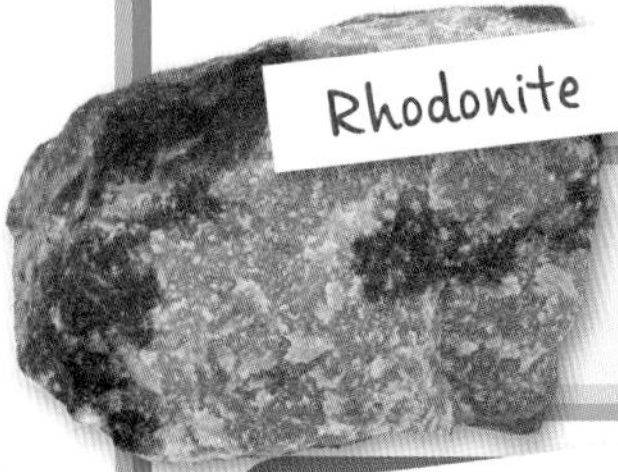

COLOUR
Rhodonite

Rocks and minerals can be a huge range of colours. Record their colours using words like 'pale', 'dark', 'streaky' or 'spotty'. The mineral rhodonite is usually described as 'bright pink' or 'rose red'.

LUSTRE
Pyrite

This is the way light bounces or reflects off a rock or mineral's surface. If hardly any light bounces off, it is 'dull'. Other terms describe common appearances like 'waxy', 'silky', 'milky' and 'vitreous' (glassy). The mineral pyrite, or fool's gold, has a 'metallic' lustre.

GRAINS AND CRYSTALS
Cerussite

Grains are small pieces in a rock or mineral. They may be 'fine' (just big enough to see), 'medium' (0.5–5 mm) or 'coarse' (over 5 mm). Grains may be rough and lumpy, or recognizable crystals with flat faces and sharp edges and corners. Sometimes there are large crystals with smaller grains around, as in the mineral cerussite.

CLEAVAGE
Galena

This describes how a rock or mineral splits or breaks along natural layers or lines, called 'fractures'. The mineral galena, an important source of lead, can cleave into box-shaped cubes.

WEIGHT
Peridotite

The rock pumice is so light it floats on water. One of the heaviest rocks is peridotite, which is carved into paperweights and scale-balance weights.

TRANSPARENCY
Garnet

If a substance is easily seen through it is 'transparent'. Misty-looking is 'translucent', and no light passing through is 'opaque'. Some rocks and minerals, like garnet, become translucent when they are cut into thin wafers.

HARDNESS

This is usually described by the Mohs scale, shown opposite.

4

PLACES TO GO

There are many great places to see and collect rocks and minerals. You can learn so much about the natural world, its habitats and wildlife, and about buildings, bridges and other constructions.

Museums have exciting displays about local rocks and fossils.

WHERE TO LOOK

Keen 'rockhounds' find rocks and minerals almost everywhere. Here are some ideas.

- A local museum with rocks and minerals from the area. Those on display will be labelled so you can start to recognize and learn about them.
- Shops that sell fossils, minerals, gemstones and interesting rock specimens.
- Rocky places near hillsides and cliffs, and seashores with boulders, pebbles and shingle.
- Stone buildings, walls, floors, patios and pavements.
- Statues, wall carvings and similar stone items.

MOHS SCALE OF HARDNESS

Each mineral on the scale will scratch the one above it, but not the one below. The second table shows common materials that can be conveniently used for comparison.

NUMBER	EXAMPLE MINERAL
1	Talc
2	Gypsum
3	Calcite
4	Fluorite
5	Apatite
6	Orthoclase
7	Quartz
8	Topaz
9	Corundum
10	Diamond

NUMBER	COMMON MATERIALS
2 ½	Fingernail
3 ½	Copper coin
5 ½	Knife blade
6	Glass
7	Hardened steel file
9	Sandpaper

STAY SAFE

Some places for finding rocks and minerals can be dangerous. Take extra care and remember:

- Always go with an experienced adult.
- Take proper clothing and equipment.
- Get permission to go on private land, and to collect specimens on protected land.
- Stay away from cliff bases, steep slopes, loose rocks, deep water and other hazards.
- Avoid wet weather as rocks will be slippery.
- On seashores, keep an eye on the tide so you don't get cut off, and beware of big waves.
- Put litter in bins or take it home.

ALBITE

The feldspar group of silica-based minerals are extremely common, especially in igneous rocks. They form more than half of all the rocks in the Earth's crust. Albite is usually bright white or clear crystals, often with tiny stripes or grooves on the flat crystal surface. Other forms of feldspar include orthoclase (page 20).

(page 20)

FACT FILE

Colour White, pale grey, perhaps lightly tinted with red, green or blue

Lustre Glassy, pearly

Crystals Shaped like bent or squashed boxes (triclinic)

Cleavage Often splits well along its flat surface

Weight Medium-heavy

Transparency Translucent or transparent

Hardness Mohs scale 6–6½

Compared to similar minerals, albite forms crystals very slowly. Large specimens that can be polished to a lustre that is slightly shinier than pearl are much desired by mineral collectors.

often bright white in colour

tiny stripes like a vinyl record groove

fracture lines have ice-like appearance

APATITE

Apatite is regarded as a mineral group based on the chemical calcium phosphate. There are varying amounts of fluoride (F), chloride (Cl), hydroxyl (OH) or other substances. The hydroxyl form, called hydroxyapatite, is an important mineral in living materials, such as bone and tooth enamel. Attractively coloured, clear specimens of apatite can be used as gems, although they are not especially hard-wearing.

Rocks rich in apatite are quarried and mined for the substance phosphorus, which is an important part of many plant fertilizers.

hard, heavy texture

blue colour due to trace elements

crystals merged and intergrown

individual crystals are different shades of colour

7

AUGITE

Like quartz (page 22), augite is in the silicate mineral group. It also contains aluminium and a variety of other metals, such as calcium, iron and tin. It is usually dark grey or green, dull-looking and heavy, but it may form large, box-shaped or many-sided crystals. Augite is common in several igneous rocks, especially basalt and gabbro (pages 24 and 27).

(page 22)(pages 24 and 27)

FACT FILE

Colour Generally dark grey, green or brown, sometimes almost black, rarely pale brown, violet

Lustre Dull, less commonly with a grainy sheen

Crystals Small box-shaped or multi-sided crystals (up to eight sides), rarely as big as a thumb

Cleavage May split easily along a large crystal face, two splits are usually almost at right angles (90°)

Weight Heavy

Transparency Usually opaque, less commonly misty

Hardness Mohs scale 5½–6

Large, well-formed crystals of augite with richly dark colours can be polished to a silky shine. But it is rarely transparent enough to be a valuable gem.

dull appearance, but may have a slight stippled or grainy shine

box-shaped or angular crystals

typical green-grey colour

twinned crystals (merged as they grew)

CALCITE

Often looking more like clear or misty plastic than glass, calcite is a form of calcium carbonate. This is the same substance that makes up limestone (page 52) and animal shells. It may form large crystals, sometimes more than one metre across. Calcite is quite soft, and is the original mineral that marks out the Mohs scale 3.

(page 52)

FACT FILE

Colour Mostly white or colourless, also grey, yellow, green, red, brown, rarely black

Lustre Glassy, pearly, rarely dull

Crystals May be very large, shaped like pyramids or distorted boxes (rhombohedral)

Cleavage May split easily along a large crystal face

Weight Medium-heavy

Transparency From perfectly transparent to milky translucence

Hardness Mohs scale 3 (original defining mineral)

Calcite is an important mineral of living things. The eyes of the long-extinct trilobites each contained hundreds of small lenses of transparent crystalline calcite clustered into a dome shape.

often milky or misty

hexagonal (six-sided) crystal shape

some crystals are almost transparent

shiny plastic-like or pearly sheen

DIAMOND

Agemstone is any mineral cut and polished to look attractive as a gem or jewel. Diamond is probably the best-known gem. It is one of the most costly and the hardest natural substance. It is made of the pure chemical substance or element, carbon. Diamonds are formed deep in the Earth, a process that takes 1000 million years or more.

Both coal and diamond are forms of the element carbon. The tiniest particles, or atoms, of carbon are packed together much more closely in diamond, making it very hard and also transparent.

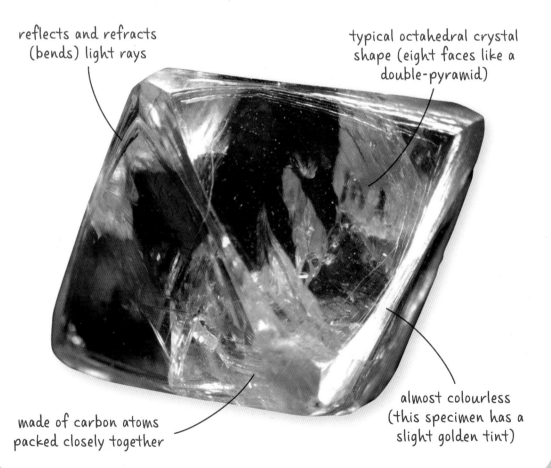

reflects and refracts (bends) light rays

typical octahedral crystal shape (eight faces like a double-pyramid)

made of carbon atoms packed closely together

almost colourless (this specimen has a slight golden tint)

FLUORITE

Also known as fluorspar, fluorite is a simple mineral containing **just calcium and fluorine.** It occurs in a wide range of bright colours, and also in a perfectly clear, colourless form like crystal glass. However it is not really hard enough to make long-lasting gems. Its crystals are typically box-shaped (cubic), but may split to form triangle-shaped corners.

Collector-quality fluorite crystals have a classic boxy shape. There is also an immense range of colours from white to black.

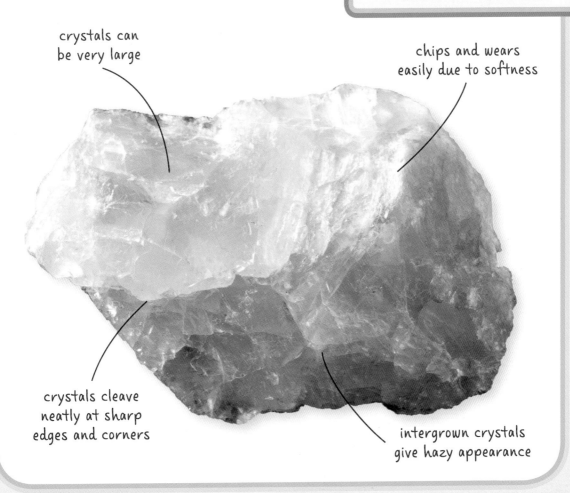

crystals can be very large

chips and wears easily due to softness

crystals cleave neatly at sharp edges and corners

intergrown crystals give hazy appearance

GYPSUM

This mineral is usually seen as large, flat crystals that are clear or milky, or in very small grains that look like soft, white or pale sand cemented into rock. Other important features of gypsum are its softness – it can be scratched by a fingernail and has a waxy, even slimy feel – and that it gradually dissolves in water.

FACT FILE

Colour Colourless, white or tinted light shades of yellow, brown, pink, blue or grey

Lustre Glassy, silky or pearly

Crystals Vary from almost too small to see in fine-grained forms, to several metres long

Cleavage May split into long, slim shards

Weight Medium

Transparency Clear to translucent, like candle wax

Hardness Mohs scale 2 (original defining mineral)

The minerals gypsum and calcite are both known as alabaster. The Alabaster Sphinx at Memphis, near Cairo, Egypt, is over 3500 years old and about 8 metres long.

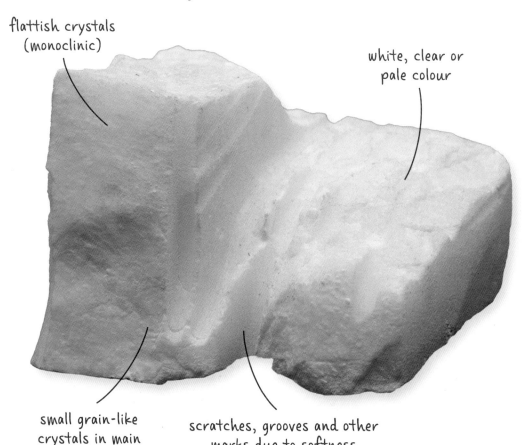

flattish crystals (monoclinic)

white, clear or pale colour

small grain-like crystals in main rock mass

scratches, grooves and other marks due to softness

HALITE

This is probably the most familiar of all minerals. People use halite for cooking, flavouring, seasoning and preserving – it is better known as common salt or rock salt, chemical name sodium chloride. Huge areas formed when ancient seas or saltwater lakes evaporated or dried, leaving the salt behind. These layers were then covered by other rocks.

FACT FILE

Colour Colourless or white, traces of other substances may cause red, pink, green or blue tinge

Lustre Glassy or vitreous

Crystals Generally box-like cubes

Cleavage Splits neatly parallel to the crystal faces

Weight Medium

Transparency May be almost perfectly transparent

Hardness Mohs scale 2–3

The town of Goderich, Ontario, Canada sits on top of a vast halite (salt) mine that is 300 metres below the surface and extends for 8 square kilometres – an area greater than the town itself.

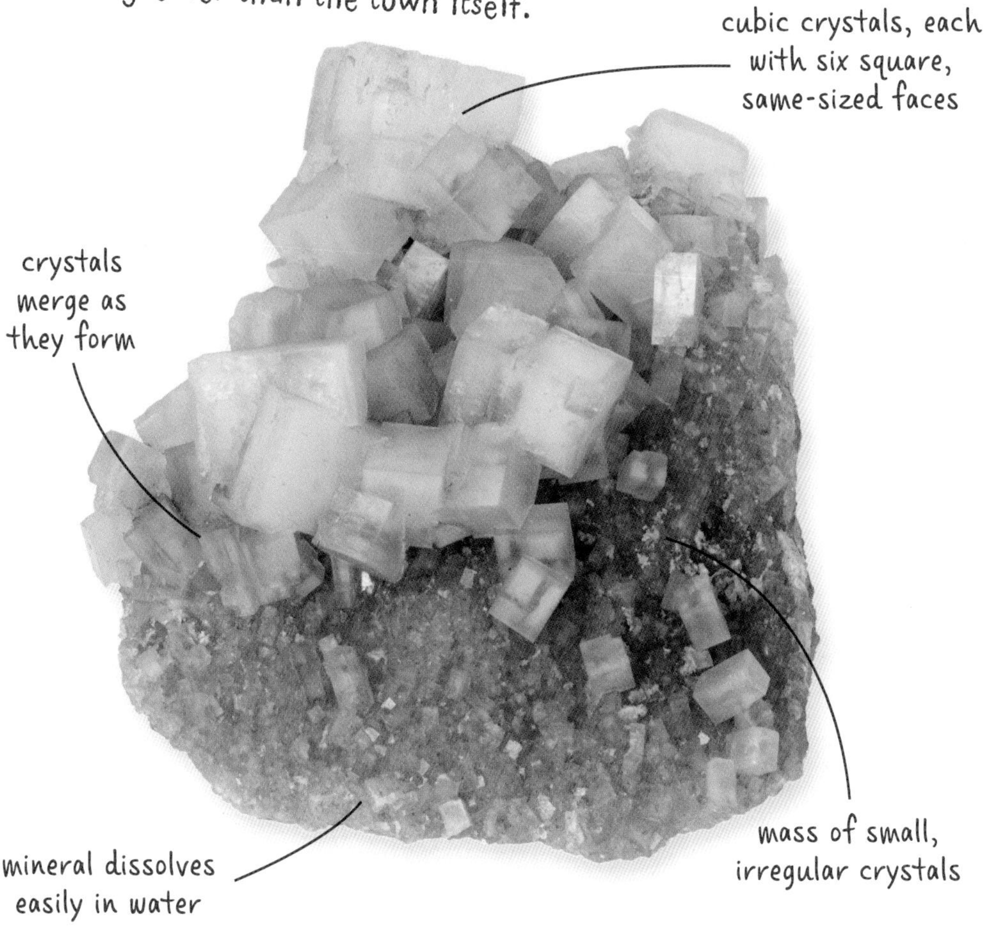

cubic crystals, each with six square, same-sized faces
crystals merge as they form
mineral dissolves easily in water
mass of small, irregular crystals

HORNBLENDE

Common in igneous and metamorphic rocks, hornblende is a group of closely similar minerals. They tend to be hard, heavy and dark – usually shades of deep green to black. Hornblende crystals can be long and slim, sometimes in bundles or sheaves. Other crystal forms are shorter and stubby.

Hornblende is among several kinds of minerals and rocks that are cut and polished as 'black granite'. They are used for walls and worktops, especially if a greenish tinge is required.

bundle of long slim crystals

dull appearance

typical dark, uneven, speckled colours

rough, broken surfaces

JADEITE

Pyroxenes are common minerals containing silicon, oxygen and aluminium, plus other metals like iron, calcium or sodium. One of the most distinctive is jadeite. Typically light to dark green, it can be worked and polished as jade to produce beautiful shiny items. Other pyroxene minerals are augite (page 8), enstatite and ferrosilite.

FACT FILE

Colour Shades of green, from pale to intense emerald-like tones, sometimes green-blue

Lustre Pearly or glassy

Crystals Rare, usually very small, indistinct, slab-like

Cleavage Uneven

Weight Heavy

Transparency Opaque, rarely translucent

Hardness Mohs scale 6½–7

Much prized through history, especially in Eastern countries, jade has been carved into many different kinds of objects, from suits of armour to vases, ornaments and sculptures.

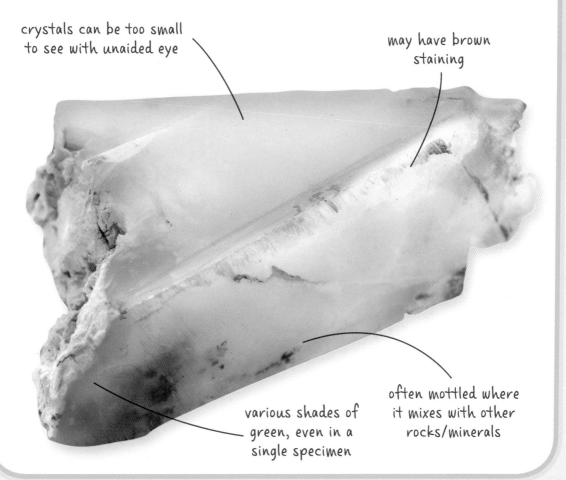

crystals can be too small to see with unaided eye

may have brown staining

various shades of green, even in a single specimen

often mottled where it mixes with other rocks/minerals

KAOLINITE

One of the clay minerals, kaolinite is soft and white or pale. The tiny crystal pieces form sheets or scales that often look like squashed-together powder. Some kinds of kaolinite-rich rocks, called kaolin, are soft enough to squish or crumble between the fingers. If water is added they become 'china clay', which is used in industries such as making ceramics, paint, paper and medicines.

FACT FILE

Colour White or pale hues of yellow, red, brown, blue

Lustre Pearly to dull, sometimes known as earthy

Crystals Tiny plate-like fragments

Cleavage Crystals split into sheets

Weight Medium

Transparency Usually opaque

Hardness Mohs scale 2–2½

Kaolin or 'china clay' mines cover vast areas. They provide fine material for porcelain and glazing paper. But they cause great damage to the landscape.

pale or white colour

powdery appearance, no internal features

tiny crystals or grains

soft and crumbly, marks easily

MAGNETITE

If you have a small iron or steel item handy, like a paper clip, identifying magnetite is easy – it should attract the clip towards it. Magnetite also affects the direction of a N-S compass needle. Containing lots of iron, it is the most naturally magnetic mineral. Magnetite is usually black or very dark, with tiny crystals or grains.

For at least 1000 years, magnetic compasses carved from magnetite-rich rock were used in China to detect the Earth's magnetic field. But no one knew at the time how they worked.

metallic sheen

dark or black colour

pyramid-shaped crystals

MICA

There are more than 20 kinds of mica, all based on substances called silicates, like quartz (page 22). All micas are 'foliate', which means they form in flat sheets. With care you can prise apart separate sheets. Common forms of mica are pale muscovite (with aluminium) and dark biotite (with iron and magnesium).

(page 22)

FACT FILE

Colour Pale to dark, depending on chemicals in the silicate, perhaps with faint long bands

Lustre Glassy, shiny plastic, sparkly

Crystals Medium to large

Cleavage Splits well into large, flat, slightly bendy sheets

Weight Medium to medium-heavy

Transparency Thin sheets can be fairly transparent

Hardness Mohs scale 2½–3

Tiny flakes of mica and similar materials make glittery, metallic or sparkly paint, which has a huge range of uses from make-up and nail varnish to high-shine treatments on custom cars.

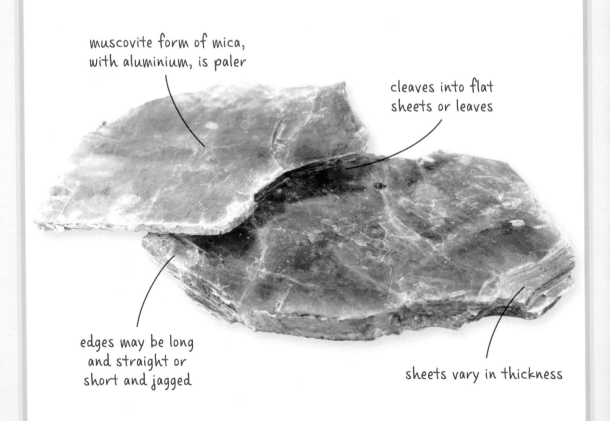

muscovite form of mica, with aluminium, is paler

cleaves into flat sheets or leaves

edges may be long and straight or short and jagged

sheets vary in thickness

OLIVINE

Named originally after its olive-green colour, olivine can also be yellow, brown or almost white. Large crystals may show faint striations (grooves, lines or steps) on their flat surfaces. Good-quality, deeply-coloured crystals are cut and polished into gems called peridot, or a lighter golden-yellow form, which is known as chrysolite.

Gem olivine, known as peridot, is August's birthstone. It varies in colour from pale yellow-green to dark olive and olive-brown. The shade depends partly on the amount of iron in the mineral.

glassy, shiny surface

many shades of green

bulky block crystals

faint lines or steps on crystal surface

ORTHOCLASE

A member of the feldspar group (see page 6), orthoclase is common in many igneous rocks, especially granite (page 28). It varies in colour but is usually light-hued, typically with box- or slab-shaped crystals that often merge together and split at right angles. It is the original mineral for Mohs scale 6.

(see page 6)
granite (page 28)

FACT FILE

Colour White or pale hues of grey, pink, yellow, green

Lustre Glassy, pearly

Crystals Box- or slab-shaped

Cleavage At right angles to form box-like edges and corners

Weight Medium to medium-heavy

Transparency Transparent to opaque

Hardness Mohs scale 6 (original defining mineral)

Faintly misty, polished forms of orthoclase and albite are known by the general name of moonstone. Ancient people regarded them as the Moon's rays turned to stone.

boxy crystal shape

merged or twinned crystals

pale or white colour

pearly appearance

PYRITE

It has a golden-yellow, metallic shine, but don't be fooled. Pyrite or 'fool's gold' has a simple chemical make-up of iron and sulphur, as iron sulphide, and contains no gold at all. It often forms box- or pyramid-shaped crystals with faintly striped or grooved faces. Striking it carefully with a steel object produces sparks.

FACT FILE

Colour Pale to darker yellow, brassy or golden, rarely silvery

Lustre Shiny, smooth surfaces reflect well when fresh, but with time become dull and tarnished

Crystals Tiny to large, box-like with flat ends (cubic) or pointed ends (octahedral)

Cleavage Uneven

Weight Very heavy

Transparency Opaque

Hardness Mohs scale 6–6½

Iron sulphide occurs in several crystal shapes. As well as pyrite, another form is marcasite, also called white iron pyrites.

faint stripes or grooves on faces of crystals

cubic or octahedral crystals

gold, yellow or brass colour

metallic shininess of fresh specimen

QUARTZ

No minerals except the feldspars are more common than quartz. It has a simple chemical make-up of just silicon and oxygen, SiO_2. Quartz is most familiar as sand grains and in sandstones (page 53), but there are also gemstone types of quartz such as yellow-brown citrine, brown-red carnelian, red jasper, purple amethyst and banded onyx.

(page 53)

FACT FILE

Colour Almost any colour from clear to black

Lustre Varies from glassy to dull

Crystals Varies from six-sided to granular

Cleavage No proper cleavage

Weight Medium-heavy

Transparency Rarely transparent, usually translucent to opaque

Hardness Mohs scale 7 (original defining mineral)

Birthstone for February, amethyst is a violet or purple form of quartz, due to traces of iron and other metals. It can be carved and polished into small delicate shapes.

large clear crystals grow and merge as they form

almost transparent

glassy appearance

six-sided crystal form

ANDESITE

Named after South America's Andes Mountains, vast amounts of this long, high range are made of andesite, where it has erupted from volcanoes over millions of years. One of the most common igneous rocks after basalt (page 24), it is usually fine-grained and brown-black, with larger pale, shiny mineral crystals, such as feldspars or biotite mica.

Andesite is one of the ore rocks mined for the metal copper. There may also be silver and perhaps gold in these mixed ores, and even the rare, costly industrial metals nickel and platinum.

basalt (page 24)

FACT FILE

Colour Brown to black, may be greenish

Appearance Fine-grained with larger, lighter crystals

Where found Andes Mountains, East Asia, Pacific Islands, Eastern Europe, Italy

Chief minerals Plagioclase feldspars (such as andesine), hornblende, pyroxene

Grains/crystals Fine grains, medium to large pale, shiny crystals

Weight Medium-heavy

Hardness Similar to Mohs scale 6–7 (5–7½)

dark, fine-grained groundmass

medium or larger, clear or pale crystals — mica or similar minerals

jagged or rough edges without neat splitting

BASALT

The most common extrusive igneous rock is basalt. 'Extrusive' means that it was formed by lava erupting, cooling and hardening. Across vast areas of the continents and much of the sea floor, 'flood basalt' forced up through enormous volcanic cracks has oozed across the surface and solidified, forming sheets. The sheets are usually dark grey to almost black with a fine, even grain.

The Giant's Causeway on the north-east coast of Ireland has many thousands of columns of basalt. They formed more than 50 million years ago by cooling after a volcanic eruption.

FACT FILE

Colour Dark grey to almost black, may be dark brown

Appearance Fine-grained, often with few or no other features, such as larger crystals

Where found North America, South Asia, Greenland, Iceland, Scotland, ocean floors, and many other places

Chief minerals Plagioclase feldspars, pyroxene

Grains/crystals Usually small and irregular, not noticeable

Weight Medium-heavy

Hardness Similar to Mohs scale 7 (5–7½)

usually dark grey in colour

fine grains and crystals too small to see easily

even appearance, larger crystals or other features are rare

does not split or cleave

DIORITE

This rock typically has a speckled or spotted appearance. Grains and crystals vary from black, through shades of grey, to almost white or colourless – there are rarely any other colours. However diorite may also be almost pure black or very pale grey. The crystals and grains vary in size from medium to coarse, with those of biotite mica perhaps giving a sparkly effect, which can be attractive.

The Code of Hammurabi stone is carved from an almost black form of diorite. More than 3700 years old and 2.2 metres tall, it lists laws and punishments for a variety of misdeeds.

FACT FILE

Colour From almost black through shades of grey to almost white

Appearance Different colours give a speckled, patchy or mottled effect

Where found Mainly Europe, Scandinavia, eastern North America, New Zealand

Chief minerals Plagioclase feldspar (such as andesine), hornblende, often biotite mica, pyroxene

Grains/crystals Mix of small, medium and larger crystals grown or interlocked together

Weight Medium-heavy

Hardness Similar to Mohs scale 5–8

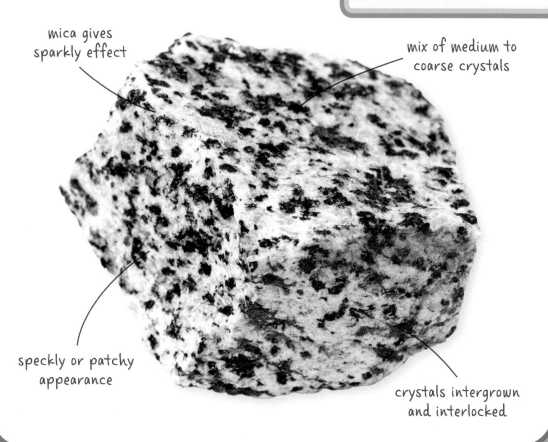

mica gives sparkly effect

mix of medium to coarse crystals

speckly or patchy appearance

crystals intergrown and interlocked

DOLERITE

Also known as diabase, dolerite **is usually dark grey or green to almost black.** It often has visible crystals from one to 5 millimetres across. Dolerite is a hard rock that erodes unevenly, so it often has a rough, scratchy texture. The main minerals are plagioclase feldspars as larger crystals, and smaller crystals of pyroxenes such as augite (page 8).

Many of the huge standing stones of Stonehenge, the famous English ancient monument built between 5000 and 4000 years ago, are dolerite.

FACT FILE

Colour Grey or green to nearly black

Appearance From dull to sparkling, may look speckled due to the different minerals

Where found On most continents, where volcanic activity has occurred in the distant past

Chief minerals Plagioclase feldspars, pyroxenes, quartz, olivine, magnetite

Grains/crystals Vary from almost too small to see without a hand lens up to 5 mm across

Weight Medium-heavy

Hardness Similar to Mohs scale 5½–7

different coloured crystals give a speckled effect

some crystals may glint or sparkle

rough, scratchy surface texture

grey colour may be slightly green-tinged due to olivine

GABBRO

Like basalt (page 24), gabbro forms huge areas under the oceans. However unlike basalt, it cooled and solidified under the Earth's surface, so it is known as 'intrusive'. This slower cooling allows large crystals to grow, which merge and interlock into a complex mass. Gabbro varies from dark to light grey, often greenish or green-grey due to the mineral olivine (page 19), perhaps with intense greenish patches.

The Cuillin Hills of Skye, Scotland, formed around 50 million years ago and consist largely of coarse-grained gabbro. The rough, angular texture gives good grip for rock climbers.

Like basalt (page 24)

FACT FILE

Colour Shades of grey from almost black to nearly white, often tinged with hues of green

Appearance Complex mass of interlocking large crystals and coarse grains

Where found Europe, especially the Alps, Greece, Turkey, also west and north Britain, western North America

Chief minerals Plagioclase feldspar, pyroxene, amphibole, olivine

Grains/crystals Medium, crystals usually at least 1–2 mm

Weight Medium-heavy

Hardness Similar to Mohs scale 5–7

various shades of colour, mainly greys

large interlocked crystals

rough, crystal-based texture

greenish tinges from olivine

GRANITE

If you find a hard, tough, pink or pink-grey rock with medium to coarse crystals or grains, perhaps tiny dark specks, and no other internal features, it is likely to be granite. There are also grey, white, yellowy and greenish types of this extremely widespread rock – one of the most common in the Earth's crust. Granite also forms some of the oldest rocks, at more than 1000 million years of age.

FACT FILE

Colour Varies from pale to dark and may be pink, grey, yellow, green and brown, even almost black

Appearance Mottled or specked appearance with pale and dark mineral crystals massed together

Where found Widespread – North America, Scandinavia, North Asia, central South America, Africa

Chief minerals Quartz, mica, feldspar

Grains/crystals Medium to coarse (usually larger than 5 mm)

Weight Medium-heavy

Hardness Similar to Mohs scale 5½–8

Sugarloaf Mountain in Rio de Janeiro, Brazil, is a rounded peak of granite almost 400 metres high. Granite is usually hard and resists erosion that wears away other rocks around it.

medium to large grains and crystals

typically pinky, speckled with black

layering may be marked

OBSIDIAN

Another name for obsidian is **'black glass'.** It is a rock that comes out of volcanoes as thick lava and cools so fast that its crystals have almost no time to grow. It cracks with scoop-like curved faces that may have circular lines and very sharp edges. Obsidian has been used since prehistory for weapons and tools such as arrowheads and axe-heads, and for shiny black ornaments and carvings.

For thousands of years obsidian has been used for arrowheads and other shard-edged weapons and tools, both for practical use and for ceremonies due to their dark, glistening beauty.

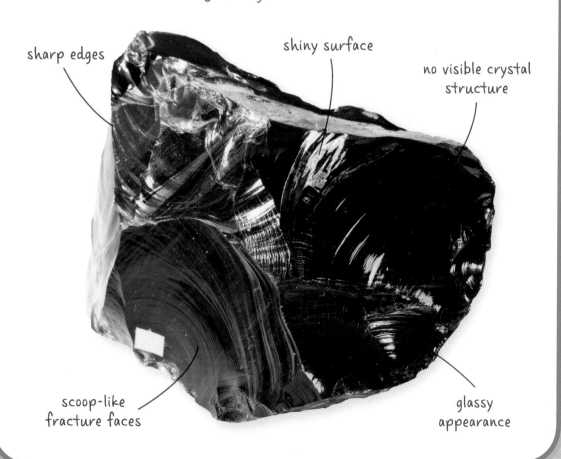

sharp edges

shiny surface

no visible crystal structure

scoop-like fracture faces

glassy appearance

PEGMATITE

A striking feature of pegmatite is its very large crystals of feldspars, quartz (page 22) and other minerals, often thumb-sized or bigger. This is due to very slow cooling and solidifying under the Earth's surface. It makes pegmatite a good source of gemstone-quality crystals of many kinds including apatite, aquamarine, clear beryl and topaz.

FACT FILE

Colour Varies from white to black with shades and colours in-between, depending on mineral make-up

Appearance Big crystals that have merged give a mixed-up, 'blocky' appearance

Where found Eastern and Southwest North America, central South America, Northern Asia, Madagascar, Australia

Chief minerals Feldspar, quartz, mica

Grains/crystals Coarse to huge, crystals grow together and merge but some may be over 5 cm across

Weight Medium to medium-heavy

Hardness Varies greatly according to minerals, usually similar to Mohs scale 6–8

Pegmatite yields a variety of gem-quality minerals that can be cut and polished as jewellery, such as topaz, which is the traditional birthstone for November.

very large, coarse crystals

'blocky' random crystal arrangement

black magnetite

crystals of different minerals are diffent colours

PORPHYRY

The general rock term 'porphyry' describes a very fine-grained mass of rock with no apparent structure, called matrix or groundmass, in which are embedded much larger crystals. These much larger crystals are known as phenocrysts. In quartz porphyry, the phenocrysts are made of the mineral quartz.

A rocky Mediterranean islet near Saint Raphael, on the south-east coast of France, is formed mainly from red porphyry rocks containing quartz and similar larger crystals.

fine groundmass

larger embedded crystals

usually grey or pinky colour

phenocryst colour depends on variety of quartz

PUMICE

There really is a rock that floats – **pumice**. It forms when lava suddenly erupts from a volcano and, with the pressure release, the tiny amounts of gas in it grow into larger bubbles (like opening a fizzy drink bottle). The rock goes 'frothy' then cools and hardens around the gas bubbles to produce a sponge-like appearance.

FACT FILE

Colour Usually pale pink, yellow, grey

Appearance Many variable-sized holes or vesicles

Where found Volcanic areas such as Italy, Southeast Asia, Japan

Chief minerals Quartz and other silicate minerals, extras such as calcite

Grains/crystals Fine, even microscopic

Weight Very light to light

Hardness Depends on amounts of bubbles, can be similar to Mohs scale 2–4

The Pantheon temple in Rome, Italy, was constructed nearly 1900 years ago. Its dome was made of an early type of concrete that had pumice fragments as its main ingredient.

porous consistency with air holes

rock around the holes is fine-grained, even frosted or glassy

colour usually pale

RHYOLITE

Similar in mineral composition to granite, rhyolite is formed when thick, viscous lava oozes from a volcano and cools rapidly. This is similar to the events that form obsidian and pumice (pages 29 and 32). Rhyolite is usually pale in colour and may have a porphyritic structure, which is a very fine-grained or glassy matrix in which are set large crystals called phenocrysts.

Plentiful outcrops of rhyolite gave their name to Rhyolite, Nevada, USA. It boomed in a brief gold rush between 1905 and 1920 and has since been a deserted 'ghost town'.

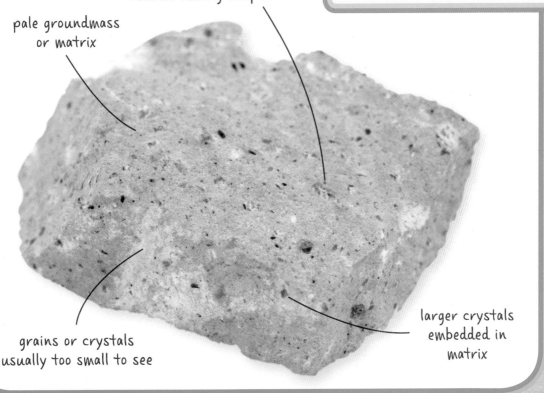

air holes or vesicles formed as air expanded after pressure release during eruption

pale groundmass or matrix

grains or crystals usually too small to see

larger crystals embedded in matrix

TUFF

Tuff is basically the ash from an erupted volcano that has been consolidated, or turned into solid rock. Ash is usually regarded as small fragments or particles, 2 millimetres or less, that are thrown into the air and then settle. Consolidation can happen in several ways, such as the particles being so hot they 'weld' together, or water that contains minerals which act like cement to bind the particles.

In Rome, Italy, many buildings both ancient and modern are made of tuff blocks from local quarries, including much of the 55,000-seater Coliseum stadium.

FACT FILE

Colour Most kinds are pale colours such as cream, light yellow, light pink or pale grey

Appearance Often lumpy and uneven, like knobbly badly-mixed concrete

Where found Areas with volcanoes, either active or extinct, including New Zealand, Indonesia, Japan, Pacific Islands, western North and South America, Italy, Greece, Turkey

Chief minerals Vary according to the type of magma that exploded out of the volcano, for example, rhyolite or andesite

Grains/crystals Fine particles about the size of sand grains, often mixed with larger lumps and pieces

Weight Medium-light

Hardness Similar to Mohs scale 4–6

texture similar to sand grains

pale colours depending on the minerals contained

lumpy, uneven formations

volcanic ash particles cemented together

GNEISS

This rock has coloured bands, which often alternate between dark and light. They may look like layers of sedimentary rocks, but in gneiss they form due to pressure and heat, which alter and move the original rock minerals into a stripy pattern that cracks roughly along the layers. Quartz (page 22) and feldspars make up the lighter bands, and iron, magnesium or similar metals in minerals form the darker ones.

The 1.7–metre–tall statue of Egyptian ruler Khafre was carved more than 4500 years ago from anorthosite gneiss. A rock related to diorite, it was brought from a quarry 600 kilometres away.

FACT FILE

Colour Light to dark, usually browns or greys

Appearance Striped or banded when seen from the side, or sheet-like when viewed from above

Where found Most areas including European Alps, Europe, North America, New Zealand, East Asia

Chief minerals Feldspars, quartz, micas

Grains/crystals Medium to coarse, in light-dark layers

Weight Medium-heavy

Hardness Similar to Mohs scale 6½–7½

large crystals

banded patterns

shades of brown, pink and grey predominate

splits along layers

HORNFELS

The hornfels group of rocks vary in their mineral make-up depending on whether they were formed originally from **sedimentary or igneous rocks.** They are usually hard, heavy, smooth lumps that are difficult to split or crack, with mixed darker colours such as greys, greens and browns, occasionally almost black. There may be lighter and darker streaks, and fine, interwoven lines.

The spectacular cliffs near Hagi, Japan, display hornfels and other rocks in banded patterns. The cliffs were formed by a huge crack, or fault, in the Earth's outer layer, the crust.

generally dark, perhaps with lighter areas

very small or no grains visible to naked eye

blue azurite mineral

smooth, hard feel

green malachite mineral

MARBLE

One of the most famous rocks, marble is made from limestone (page 52) that has been subjected to great heat, but only low pressure. Its pure form is almost white, but different minerals can give it a wide range of colours, from palest pink or blue to dark grey and brown. Look closely in strong light to see how marble's tiny crystals sparkle.

The Taj Mahal near Agra, India, was completed around 1650. It is a magnificent tomb, or mausoleum, built of white marble, with the main dome reaching a height of 35 metres.

(page 52)

FACT FILE

Colour From white to pale grey, blue, brown, green, pink, violet

Appearance Pearly or silky, polishes to a high shine

Where found Famously in Italy, but many other areas such as China, Spain, India, Britain, North America

Chief minerals Calcite, dolomite, small amounts of many others

Grains/crystals Fine to coarse

Weight Medium to medium-heavy

Hardness Similar to Mohs scale 3–4 (rarely 2–5)

other minerals give colours — pink is caused by iron minerals such as haematite or goethite

amorphous (no internal layers, blocks or other structures)

main crystals are usually calcite and dolomite

crystals interlock as a solid mass

PHYLLITE

This rock is made from other metamorphic rocks, such as slate (page 42), that have undergone further changes as a result of heat and pressure. Phyllite tends to form in sheet-like layers that can be as thin as paper or thicker than bricks, and which may be flat, wavy or wrinkled. The rock is usually some shade of grey, perhaps tinged green by the mineral chlorite, and the mineral mica's tiny flakes give it a silky sheen.

The Gandhara style of art originated in north-west Pakistan almost 2000 years ago, and often featured greenish phyllite stone.

FACT FILE

Colour Pale to darker grey, may be tinged with green

Appearance Layered or leaved, although does not spilt easily, can look silvery or silky due to tiny mica flakes

Where found Europe, especially the Alps and western Isles of Scotland, eastern North America, small amounts in many other areas

Chief minerals Quartz, sericite mica, chlorite, feldspars

Grains/crystals Fine to medium grains, flake-like particles of mica

Weight Medium to heavy

Hardness Similar to Mohs scale 2–4

silky sheen

greenish tinge

fine to medium grain

layers are wavy or crinkly

QUARTZITE

As its name suggests, this rock contains lots of the mineral quartz (page 22). Mostly it forms from sandstone (page 53) that has been heated and squashed, causing the original grains to break down (but not melt) and merge together. This sometimes gives quartzite a glassy appearance. The heat and pressure also remove the original grains and features, such as layers and fossils.

Quartzite's hardness, weather resistance and attractive colours mean it is a popular choice for sea walls to protect coasts from wearing away or erosion.

FACT FILE

Colour White, pale to dark grey, pink, red or brown due to iron minerals

Appearance Sandpapery to smooth mix of tiny grains of various shades, may glint due to mica

Where found Widespread, including North America, Britain, central South America, Southeast Africa

Chief minerals Quartz, micas, feldspars

Grains/crystals Medium to very fine, sometimes invisible

Weight Medium-heavy

Hardness Similar to Mohs scale 6½–7½

pale colours in various shades

sheen and glinting appearance

layers have persisted in this specimen

very small fine grains

SCHIST

The schist group of rocks are typically flaky, scaly or leafy, because of minerals such as biotite or muscovite micas (page 18). This feature of splitting easily into thin, flat pieces (cleavage) is known as 'foliated'. Different types of schist are named after their typical minerals or appearance such as mica schist, chlorite schist and garnet schist. Green schist is shown here.

In the great Mount Rushmore carvings of US presidents in South Dakota, the main rock is granite. However, darker schist is visible below President George Washington on the far left.

FACT FILE

Colour Varies greatly according to mineral make-up, from white to black, also greenish, yellow, pink, red, blue

Appearance Flaky or scaly, micas give a sheen, layers may be folded

Where found Very widespread on every continent, especially in mountainous areas

Chief minerals Variable, including micas, chlorite, graphite, hornblende, quartz

Grains/crystals Flat, scaly pieces that split easily

Weight Medium-heavy

Hardness Similar to Mohs scale 4–6½

varied colours depending on minerals such as chlorite, serpentine and epidote

shiny or sheen-like gleam

layers of splitting

SERPENTINITE

The name serpentinite is given to several kinds of rocks that contain minerals in the serpentine group. These include chrysotile and antigorite (white asbestos), plus other non-serpentine minerals, like olivine (page 19). It is usually green, varying from pale green to deep greenish-black, with chunky, medium-sized to coarse crystals, varying from the size of rice grains to grapes. These features make it prized for carving and polishing.

Serpentinite is the official rock of California, USA. It is also used in nuclear power stations since it is good at blocking dangerous rays and radiation.

FACT FILE

Colour Greenish, from pale to very dark, often in patches of different shades, sometimes with red zones (areas)

Appearance May be banded, veined or zoned, sometimes with fibre-like bundles, often a greasy or waxy sheen

Where found Widespread, including European Alps, Britain, east and west North America, eastern Australia, New Zealand, Caribbean islands

Chief minerals Serpentine minerals such as antigorite, chrysotile, lizardite and many others

Grains/crystals Medium to coarse, usually in clumps or patches

Weight Medium

Hardness Similar to Mohs scale 2–4

green patches of different shades

zones or banding

medium to large crystals

fibrous bundles

SLATE

Usually grey with a waxy or greasy sheen, slate is formed by heat and pressure acting on sedimentary rocks such as mudstone and shale (page 54). It is famous for splitting into large, thin, flat sheets. For centuries these sheets have been made into 'slates' on roofs and old-fashioned tablets or blackboards to be written on with chalk. Slate may contain fossil traces from the original rock.

'Slates' are flat tiles made of slate rock. They have been used for roofing for thousands of years. Highly polished decorative types of slates are put on walls and floors.

FACT FILE

Colour Usually a shade of grey, perhaps with light or dark spots, streaks, lines or veins, can be tinged blue, green or red

Appearance Fine-grained waxy or silky sheen, perhaps with lumps or nodules of other minerals

Where found Famous slate quarries exist in Britain, northern, central and western Europe, North and South America, and other regions

Chief minerals Depends on original rock, usually quartz, feldspars, micas, clay minerals

Grains/crystals Fine-grained

Weight Medium-heavy

Hardness Variable, similar to Mohs scale 3–5½

fine, grey grains

sheet-like splitting planes

streaks or lumps of other minerals

SOAPSTONE

Also known as steatite, soapstone **is one of several rocks that are easier to recognize by touch rather than looks.** It has a soft, 'soapy' feel – not wet or moist, but rather slippery or slick. This is because it is mainly talc, one of the softest of all minerals, with a whitish colour. Other minerals include magnetite (page 17), which gives grey hues and chlorite (greenish).

Soapstone forms the outer layer of the famous mountaintop statue called Christ the Redeemer, which towers over the Brazilian city of Rio de Janeiro.

FACT FILE

Colour Ranges from creamy white through pale green, grey and brown, to darker shades of green or grey

Appearance Silky or pearl-like surface, can be slightly translucent

Where found On most continents, especially North America, Scandinavia, East Africa, South and East Asia, Brazil

Chief minerals Usually at least four-fifths talc, also magnetite, chlorite and dolomite

Grains/crystals Fine grains or particles, larger crystals are very rare

Weight Medium

Hardness Similar to Mohs scale 1–2 (rarely 2½)

greenish coloration due to chlorite mineral

silky or waxen appearance

soft, soapy, 'greasy' feel

BRECCIA

Like conglomerate (page 47), breccia consists of a fine-grained matrix or groundmass containing medium or larger lumps of other rocks. However, unlike conglomerate, these lumps, called clasts, are angular or sharp-edged. Breccia forms when rocky bits of cliffs break off in rockslides, cliff falls or avalanches. The bits collect in fine-grained sediments, which gradually harden.

The Cinchado Rock is on the island of Tenerife, off the north-west coast of Africa. It is an outcrop of breccia that still stands, while the surrounding softer rocks have worn away.

(page 47)

unworn lumps have angles, edges and points

larger, lumpy material stands out

fine-grained matrix

FACT FILE

Colour Lumps depend on type of original rock, but matrix is usually light, such as cream, grey, yellow

Appearance Angular rock pieces with points and edges, set in natural 'cement'

Where found Widespread around the world, but usually in small quantities

Chief minerals Depends on original rock, but matrix can be quartz, clay minerals, calcite, salt minerals

Particles Large, angular lumps usually more than 5 mm across

Weight Medium to heavy

Hardness Depends on original rock, similar to Mohs scale 5–8

CHALK

A form of limestone (page 52), chalk is easily recognized as a bright white, fairly soft or even powdery rock. It is porous, which means it is able to soak up lots of water or other liquid. Chalk is mostly made up of the mineral calcite (page 9), and it formed from the shells and body coverings (exoskeletons) of dead sea creatures that sank to the ocean floor millions of years ago.

Good-quality chalk is quarried for use in a huge range of industries and products from cement and concrete to toothpaste and cosmetics.

(page 52)
(page 9)

FACT FILE

Colour White, perhaps tinged with pale yellow, pink or blue

Appearance Fine-grained and powdery texture, may feel hard and solid or so soft it crumbles in the hand

Where found Common across Europe, also occurs less commonly in most other regions

Chief minerals Calcite, silt and clay minerals

Particles Fine to powder-like

Weight Medium-light to medium-heavy

Hardness Varies, similar to Mohs scale 2–4

white or almost white colour

fine-grained, powdery appearance

no clear layering

relatively soft, easily grooved and worn

COAL

This rock formed over millions of years, when huge swampy areas of plant matter died, and was buried and compacted to form fossil-based material. Its main substance is carbon from those plants. Depending on how far advanced the changes are, coal can be softer and brown as lignite, black with a sheen as bituminous coal, or hard, black and glossy as anthracite (one type of domestic coal).

Coal-mining is one of the world's biggest industries. Burning coal in power stations provides one quarter of our power, but it releases harmful gases into the Earth's atmosphere.

FACT FILE

Colour Brown to jet-black

Appearance Dull to shiny, breaks into irregular, flat areas

Where found Many areas on all continents, with large amounts mined for fuel

Chief minerals Main substance is carbon, but also nitrogen, sulphur and others

Particles May have tiny crystals

Weight Light (bituminous) to medium (anthracite)

Hardness Similar to Mohs scale 2–4

black colour

broken ridges and faces

may contain fossils or fossil-like formations

shiny surface

CONGLOMERATE

Similar to breccia (page 44), conglomerate has lumps of rock called clasts in a grainy surround or matrix. However, its clasts are worn and rounded, like beach pebbles, rather than sharp-edged and pointed. Conglomerate forms on sea beds, river banks, flood plains and similar places where clasts are worn, tumbled and rounded.

FACT FILE

Colour Lumps depend on type of original rock but matrix is usually light, such as cream, grey, pale yellow

Appearance Rounded clasts (rock pieces) set in natural 'cement'

Where found Widespread around the world, but usually in small quantities

Chief minerals Depends on original rock, but matrix can be quartz, clay minerals, calcite, salt minerals

Particles Clasts are usually more than 5 mm across

Weight Medium to heavy

Hardness Depends on original rock, similar to Mohs scale 5–8

Conglomerate rocks have been found on Mars, which is evidence that water once existed on the 'Red Planet'.

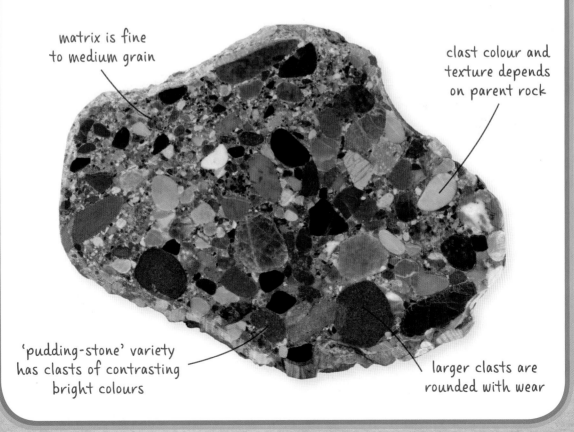

matrix is fine to medium grain

clast colour and texture depends on parent rock

'pudding-stone' variety has clasts of contrasting bright colours

larger clasts are rounded with wear

DOLOMITE

This rock is also called dolostone, to avoid confusion with the mineral also known as dolomite. The rock dolomite contains large amounts of the mineral dolomite, which is made mainly of calcium carbonate and magnesium carbonate. It is similar in some ways to limestone (page 52), but harder and heavier. This rock is named from the Dolomite Mountains of Italy where it is very common.

(page 52)

FACT FILE

Colour Light grey or brown, occasionally yellow or pink

Appearance Evenly arranged grains, with few traces of layering or other patterns or structures

Where found Most regions, especially where rocks are very old (Cambrian, over 500 million years)

Chief minerals Dolomite, calcite, also small amounts of quartz and pyrite

Particles Small, same-size grains

Weight Medium-heavy

Hardness Similar to Mohs scale 3–5

Explorers for oil and gas are usually pleased to find dolomite, since its tiny holes or pores often fill with natural gas or petroleum oil.

small grains regularly arranged

usually pale to medium grey or brown in colour

even texture with few marks or features

may emit a fetid (rotten or putrid) smell when struck

FLINT

This rock is usually found with other rocks, such as chalk (page 45), as nodules (lumps). These nodules can range in size from smaller than a pea to bigger than a football, and may have smooth and broken areas, with very tiny crystals inside. Chert is similar to flint, but with slightly larger grains. Chalcedony is also similar, but contains the mineral moganite, with a slightly different crystal shape.

(page 45)

FACT FILE

Colour Variable, pale yellow or grey to almost black, sometimes with zones or bands inside

Appearance Knobbly lumps, nodules or sheets

Where found Europe, North America, many other regions especially with chalks and other limestones

Chief minerals Quartz and others

Particles Tiny, even microscopic, crystals

Weight Medium

Hardness Similar to Mohs scale 7

Flint was an ideal Stone Age material to chip and fashion into arrowheads, spearheads, scrapers, choppers and similar sharp items. This process, called knapping, requires great skill.

lumpy, uneven form

may have ripples, grooves, bands or zones inside

crystals too small to see

other minerals form patchy areas

sharp-edged chips and cracks

FOSSILS

Fossils are usually hard parts of living things that were buried in sediments, preserved, and gradually turned to rock over millions of years. Since this process often happened in water, the most common fossils are of sea creatures, especially those that had hard shells. Other things that have been fossilized include bark, cones, nuts, and animal shells, teeth, bones and claws.

The biggest fossils are limb bones of huge dinosaurs like the 60-tonne, 26-metre *Dreadnoughtus*, perhaps the biggest-ever dinosaur, announced in 2014.

fossil ammonite (extinct shelled sea creature, relative of today's octopus and squid)

surrounding rock or matrix is limestone

ribs of shell stand out

animal's head and tentacles protruded from wide end

fossil is also made of limestone

IRONSTONE

A hard, heavy rock that has a 'rusty' appearance may well be ironstone. The rust is reddish, orange or brown iron oxide, formed when the iron in iron-rich minerals reacts with oxygen in the air, in the presence of water vapour (moisture). Several types of rocks contain enough iron-based minerals to be known as ironstone, such as shales (page 54) and mudstones.

Ironstone was an important ore rock (source) for iron as the Industrial Revolution started in the 1700s. But supplies soon ran low and hematite, magnetite and other ores took over.

freshly exposed surface is usually grey

colours vary from yellow-orange through red to brown

rust-like patches form on exposure to air

51

LIMESTONE

This rock is basically the mineral calcite (page 9), a form of calcium carbonate, usually with bits and pieces from sea creatures, broken into various sizes. Limestone may be fine-grained with tiny particles, or coarse with whole fossil shells and similar items. There are many types of limestone, depending on what it contains – coralline limestone has remains of corals, shelly limestone has shells, and so on.

Many of Egypt's ancient pyramids were built of limestone. The biggest, the Great Pyramid of Khufu at Giza, has over 5 million tonnes of limestone blocks.

FACT FILE

Colour Usually light – cream, grey, yellowish to brown, but many other colours too

Appearance Fine matrix 'cement' containing fossils that may be whole or broken into small fragments

Where found Worldwide in many different forms

Chief minerals Calcite, aragonite, plus many others like quartz

Particles Grain size varies with types of fragments from original rock and living things

Weight Medium-heavy

Hardness Variable according to make-up, similar to Mohs scale 3–6

possible remains of fossils, or whole fossils may be visible

variable grain size

calcite crystals can give a sparkle or gleam

mottled or patchy appearance

SANDSTONE

Sand comes in many colours, from almost white to yellow, pink, red, brown, grey and nearly black. So sandstone, made of sand grains squeezed and 'cemented' together, can be these colours too. Sandstone may show strata (layers) where different grains settled at different times in a sea, lake or riverbank. The same kind of layering takes place with loose, windblown grains in a desert.

FACT FILE

Colour Almost white, yellow, pink to red, brown, shades of green and grey, nearly black

Appearance Usually an even, grainy, sandpapery look, may contain rocky pieces and fossils, micas may give slight sparkle

Where found Worldwide in many different forms

Chief minerals Quartz, feldspars, sometimes micas

Particles Grains are sand-sized (officially 0.06–2 mm)

Weight Medium

Hardness Similar to Mohs scale 6–7½

The Wave rock formation in Arizona, USA, has been eroded and smoothed by windblown sand, dust and rain over millions of years, revealing multi-coloured layers of sandstone.

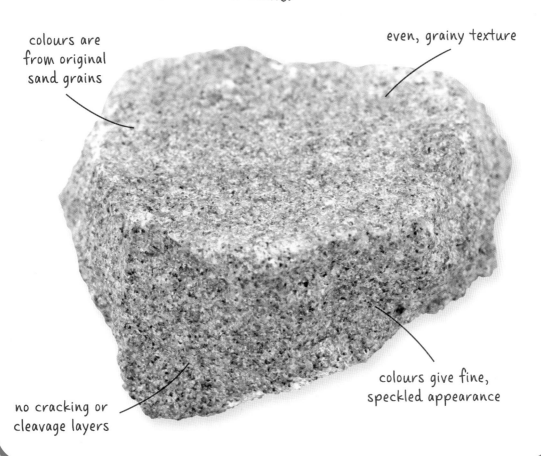

colours are from original sand grains

even, grainy texture

no cracking or cleavage layers

colours give fine, speckled appearance

SHALE

This is rock formed from clay-type minerals in silt and mud that settled on sea and lake beds millions of years ago and hardened. Shale is usually dark with grains too small to see. It has laminations (thin layers) that break into flat, angle-edged pieces with ridges and grooves. Mudstones and siltstones are similar but split less easily.

Shale rocks contain vast amounts of natural gas and oil. New methods of drilling and 'fracking' in shales have hugely increased supplies of these fossil fuels.

grains too small to see

usually dark grey colour

may glint slightly

may contain flattened fossils

METEORITES

Meteorites are rocks from space that do not burn up as 'shooting stars' and so crash onto the Earth's surface. Most contain tiny rounded particles called chondrules, which look like glass beads. A few contain iron, so a magnet may stick to them. There may be a 'fusion crust' covering, due to great heat and burning in the atmosphere, and bowl-like areas separated by ridges, like miniature mountains and valleys.

The Hoba meteorite in Namibia, Africa, is the world's biggest. It probably fell more than 50,000 years ago and still lies in the same place. The meteorite weighs about 60 tonnes.

FACT FILE

Colour Very variable, usually mid-grey or brown to black

Appearance Variable, may have a blackened crust, with edges and hollows that look like they have been melted

Where found Worldwide

Chief minerals Usually silica-containing minerals, also iron minerals

Grains/crystals Many have chondrules (rounded particles) from about 0.2–10 mm across

Weight Medium to heavy

Hardness Similar to Mohs scale 4–8

yellow, grey and brown are common colours

scoops and hollows that look like they have been melted

random shape with no inner layers or other structures

GLOSSARY

Birthstone A gem traditionally linked to the month of a person's birth, hopefully to bring good luck and happiness.

Ceramics Materials made from natural, non-metallic minerals (those that contain little or no metallic particles), especially types of clay that have been heated or baked, and then cooled to become hard.

China clay Common name for kaolin, a soft white clay containing lots of kaolinite and similar minerals. It is used for making porcelain (fine 'china') and in many other industries.

Cleavage How a rock or mineral splits or breaks along natural layers or lines, called fractures.

Crystal A shape with flat faces called facets, that join at angled edges and pointed ends. Crystal shapes vary from very simple, like a box-shaped cube, to multisided pyramids and columns.

Cubic A crystal that is shaped like a box with six sides, eight corners and 12 edges.

Extrusive rock Igneous rock that reaches the Earth's surface as lava, cools and turns solid there.

Foliate In the form of many similar sheets or leaves piled on top of each other.

Gemstone (Gem) Any mineral that can be cut, polished or otherwise prepared so that it is valuable, because of its colour, sparkle, rarity, or another sought-after feature.

Groundmass Another name for the matrix, the fine-grained material in which larger items are found. Often groundmass has even finer grains than matrix, almost invisible even under a microscope.

Igneous rock A rock type formed when the original rock became so hot and/or pressurized that it melted, then cooled and turned solid.

Intrusive rock Igneous rock that stays beneath the Earth's surface as magma, cools and turns solid there.

Lava Very hot, molten (melted) rock that came from deep in the Earth onto the surface in a volcanic eruption.

Lustre The way light bounces or reflects off a rock or mineral's surface, for example, dull, waxy or vitreous (glassy).

Magma Very hot, molten (melted) rock deep in the Earth, below the surface. It is called lava if it comes onto the surface.

Matrix The fine-grained material, or even lacking any grainy texture at all, in which larger items are set or embedded.

Metamorphic rock A rock type formed when the original rock became so pressurized and hot (but not melted) that it changed the form of its crystals or grains.

Mohs scale A 1–10 scale (measure) of the hardness of a mineral, by comparing it with a list of ten minerals originally used to define each number. 1 (softest) is talc, 10 (hardest) is diamond. It was devised in 1812 by German mineral expert Friedrich Mohs.

Phenocryst A larger, obvious crystal, easily identified in its fine-grained matrix.

Porous Allowing substances to soak in and pass through, usually due to a network of tiny spaces or pores, just like a sponge, which is porous to water.

Porphyry A rock type in which large, distinct crystals or similar items (phenocrysts) are set into a fine-grained matrix or groundmass.

Pyramid A shape with triangular sides that come to a point at one end, and a base with as many sides as there are triangles. Pyramids can have three sides (tetrahedron, with a triangle base), four sides (pentahedron, with a square base) or more sides.

Sedimentary rock A rock type formed when sediments (particles) settled under the force of gravity and then became pressurized, cemented by other minerals, and perhaps heated (but not melted) to form a new kind of rock.

Vesicles Small cavities, chambers, holes or similar spaces, usually rounded in shape.